SCOTNO'
Number

Robert Louis Stevenson's

Treasure Island, Kidnapped

and

Catriona

Christopher MacLachlan

School of English
University of St Andrews

Association for Scottish Literary Studies 2006

Published by
Association for Scottish Literary Studies
c/o Department of Scottish History
University of Glasgow
9 University Gardens
Glasgow G12 8QH
www.asls.org.uk

First published 2006

A CIP catalogue for this title is available from the British Library

ISBN 0-948877-73-1
ISBN-13: 978-0-948877-73-5

Subsidised by

Scottish
Arts Council

Typeset by Roger Booth Associates, Hassocks, West Sussex

CONTENTS

Page

SCOTNOTES

Study guides to major Scottish writers and literary texts

Produced by the Schools and Further Education Committee
of the Association for Scottish Literary Studies

THE ASSOCIATION FOR SCOTTISH LITERARY STUDIES aims to promote the study, teaching and writing of Scottish literature, and to further the study of the languages of Scotland.

To these ends, the ASLS publishes works of Scottish literature; literary criticism and in-depth reviews of Scottish books in *Scottish Studies Review*; short articles, features and news in *ScotLit*; and scholarly studies of language in *Scottish Language*. It also publishes *New Writing Scotland*, an annual anthology of new poetry, drama and short fiction, in Scots, English and Gaelic. ASLS has also prepared a range of teaching materials covering Scottish language and literature for use in schools.

All the above publications are available as a single 'package', in return for an annual subscription. Enquiries should be sent to: ASLS, c/o Department of Scottish History, 9 University Gardens, University of Glasgow, Glasgow G12 8QH. Telephone/fax +44 (0)141 330 5309, e-mail office@asls.org.uk or visit our website at **www.asls.org.uk**

EDITOR'S FOREWORD

The *Scotnotes* booklets are a series of study guides to major Scottish writers and literary texts that are likely to be elements within literature courses. They are aimed at senior pupils in secondary schools and students in further education colleges and colleges of education. Each booklet in the series is written by a person who is not only an authority on the particular writer or text but also experienced in teaching at the relevant levels in schools or colleges. Furthermore, the editorial board, composed of members of the Schools and Further Education Committee of the Association for Scottish Literary Studies, considers the suitability of each booklet for the students in question.

For many years there has been a shortage of readily accessible critical notes for the general student of Scottish literature. *Scotnotes* has grown as a series to meet this need, and provides students with valuable aids to the understanding and appreciation of the key writers and major texts within the Scottish literary tradition.

Lorna Borrowman Smith
Ronald Renton

A NOTE ON THE TEXTS USED IN THIS BOOK

Treasure Island and *Kidnapped* are both available in a number of editions, mainly in paperback, some very cheap. I have used the Oxford Classics (originally World's Classics) edition of *Treasure Island*, edited by Emma Letley and first published in 1985. This has a good introduction and notes, and includes Stevenson's essay 'My First Novel' about the writing of *Treasure Island*. I have also used Emma Letley's combined edition of *Kidnapped* and *Catriona* from the same publisher (1986), although this is now out of print. Unfortunately there are at present no cheap editions of *Catriona* in print. In referring to all three novels I have used chapter rather than page numbers. Locating quotations used in this book therefore means turning through the pages of a chapter but I hope that will not be too difficult, since all three novels are divided into quite short chapters.

Life of Robert Louis Stevenson

Robert Louis Stevenson was born on 13 November 1850 in Edinburgh. His father, Thomas Stevenson, was a lighthouse engineer, carrying on a family tradition of building lighthouses around the coast of Scotland. He hoped his only son would follow him in this career but from an early age Robert Louis Stevenson's health was poor. So was that of his mother and his upbringing was therefore largely in the hands of his nurse, Alison Cunningham (known as Cummie). She filled his mind with Scottish stories but, because she was also a God-fearing Calvinist, she also filled the small boy with fears of damnation which would haunt some of his adult fiction.

Stevenson's education was patchy but he did attend Edinburgh Academy for a couple of years and in 1867 he entered the University of Edinburgh, at first to study engineering but then he switched to law. He really wanted to be a writer but his parents did not regard that as a sound enough profession and insisted he take a degree in a subject which would qualify for a proper career. Though he passed his degree and became a lawyer in 1875, he did not practise law and instead turned to writing.

During this period he quarrelled with his parents over religion, shocking them by saying he doubted the existence of God. He also shocked them by deliberately adopting a Bohemian pose, that is, by dressing in a foppish manner, wearing his hair long and spending his leisure time in some of the shady parts of Edinburgh. By the middle of the 1870s, however, he was beginning to have essays published in London magazines. Stevenson's health was still not strong and because the Scottish climate was not good for him he began to spend time abroad, particularly in France. In 1876 he made a canoe trip along the canals of Belgium and northern France that resulted in his first book, *An Inland Voyage* (1878), which was well received but made little money.

Meanwhile, he had discovered the artists' colony at Grez, south of Paris, and there he met the woman he was to marry. Fanny Osbourne was an American married woman some years older than Stevenson and already had a daughter and a young son, Lloyd. Most of Stevenson's friends were against his relationship with Fanny and he kept it from his parents. She herself had doubts and went back to join her husband in California in 1878. Stevenson then set off on his famous trip through the Cevennes mountains in France with the donkey Modestine that would be the basis for his most famous travel book, *Travels with a Donkey* (1879). It is evident in that book that during the trip he thought deeply about his relationship with Fanny and, although afterwards he returned to Britain and continued his writing, in August 1879 he suddenly took ship for America and travelled by rail across the USA from New York to California to be with her. The journey, described in his book *The Amateur Emigrant*, nearly killed him and at the end he found Fanny was still undecided and still married.

Stevenson was now in dire straits. The terrible journey to California brought on the first real symptoms of the lung disease which would plague him for the rest of his life and his sudden and secret departure without telling his family meant he could no longer count on his father's financial assistance. He was also now a long way from the London literary circles which had supported his writing. In April 1880, however, his father forgave him and promised him an annual allowance of £250. About this time Fanny at last obtained a divorce and was free to marry him. After a short honeymoon Stevenson returned to Scotland with Fanny and her son Lloyd (her daughter had married and settled down in America).

From 1881 until the death of his father in 1887 Stevenson spent his time in various places in Britain and France, with spells in Davos, a health resort in Switzerland. Scotland's weather proved so dangerous to his health that he frequently spent time in the south of France and in 1884 he settled in Bournemouth in the south of England. His literary career was making some headway but he was still dependent on his father, who for instance paid for the Bournemouth house. In 1883 *Treasure Island* was published and was a great success, followed in 1885 by his volume of poems *A Child's Garden of Verses*, but Stevenson's real breakthrough as a writer came in 1886 with the publication of *The Strange Case of Dr Jekyll and Mr Hyde*, which was such a successful best-seller that after it Stevenson had no trouble finding contracts with publishers for his essays and stories. In the same year *Kidnapped* was published, further enhancing Stevenson's reputation.

When Stevenson, with his mother, Fanny and Lloyd, went to the USA in 1887 he found *Jekyll and Hyde* had made him famous. The Stevensons spent some time at Saranac Lake, near the Canadian border, where the cold winter climate was thought to be good for his lungs, but in 1888 he hired a ship and the family sailed from San Francisco on a voyage around the South Pacific, visiting many of the islands, including Tahiti and Hawaii, where they stayed for some time. Stevenson continued to write, sending essays and fiction back to London where his friend Sidney Colvin helped to get them published. In 1889 one of Stevenson's best novels, *The Master of Ballantrae*, appeared and in the same year he reached Samoa, where he bought some land. After a visit to Australia and another cruise amongst the islands of the South Pacific he returned to Samoa and built a house there. Vailima in Samoa now became his permanent home.

From 1891 until his death at the end of 1894 Stevenson worked on a number of literary projects, fiction and non-fiction, novels, tales and essays. He became very interested in the history of the South Pacific and its politics, and in fact got involved in the political situation in Samoa. He wrote *In the South Seas* (1891) about his travels and the history and customs of the islands he had visited and in *A Footnote to History* (1892) he surveyed Samoan history and politics. He also published a number of stories set in the Pacific islands, notably 'The Beach at Falesá' (1893) and 'The Ebb-Tide' (1894), but wrote about Scotland, too, publishing *Catriona*, the sequel to *Kidnapped*, in 1893 and leaving at his death two unfinished novels set in Edinburgh, *St Ives* and *Weir of Hermiston*.

Stevenson died suddenly on 3 December 1894. Next day he was buried on the top of a mountain in Samoa, where he still lies. Fanny survived him by many years, not dying until 1914, and as the author's widow she did her best to preserve Stevenson's memory and reputation, overseeing the publication of his works and the writing of an official biography. Unfortunately the image of Stevenson she wished to maintain provoked a reaction against Stevenson in the early twentieth century. Critics attacked him as a writer with more style than substance and he was relegated to the status of an author whose novels were only suitable for children. His fame was probably kept alive by the cinema. *Dr Jekyll and Mr Hyde*, *Treasure Island* and *Kidnapped* were all made into films and then television series. With the increase of academic interest in Scottish fiction in the second half of the twentieth century Stevenson took his place in the line of Scottish novelists that passes from Sir Walter Scott and James Hogg through Stevenson to John Buchan and down to today, and this has in turn fostered interest in his other works. The romance of Stevenson's life will always bring him admirers and his most popular fiction seems destined to survive even amongst those who know little else about him other than Long John Silver, Alan Breck and Jekyll and Hyde, but he is also worth attention as a poet and critic and as a highly representative figure of his time and literary period.

Treasure Island

Stevenson gives a full and vivid account of the writing of *Treasure Island* in an essay called 'My First Book', first published in 1894 and often reprinted in collections of his essays and criticism (it is included in the Oxford Classics edition of the novel, edited by Emma Letley). He began writing *Treasure Island*, under its original title *The Sea Cook*, while on holiday in late summer, 1881, partly to amuse his stepson, Lloyd Osbourne, but the rest of the family, particularly his father, also became enthusiastic followers of the story. The editor of the magazine *Young Folks*, hearing of the tale, offered to publish it as a serial, but under the now familiar title. *Treasure Island* appeared in book form in 1883 and was an immediate success, although Stevenson did not make a lot of money from it.

Outline

Apart from Chapters 16 to 18 the novel is narrated by its hero, Jim Hawkins, the teenage son of the keeper of the 'Admiral Benbow', an isolated inn on the coast of Devon in England. To it there comes a rough old seaman, Billy Bones, who takes up residence, spending his nights drinking and his days looking out to sea, as though on watch. He asks Jim to let him know if he ever sees a seafaring man with only one leg. Some time passes and then another seaman arrives asking to see Bones. There is an argument, Bones chases his visitor from the inn and then has a heart attack. Jim and Dr David Livesey, the local doctor, have to put him to bed. After a partial recovery he receives another visitor, a blind man called Pew, who gives Bones a piece of paper marked with a black spot, the signal that a pirate crew has turned against its captain. As the blind man flees Billy Bones dies of a second heart attack.

Afraid that the pirates will return, Jim and his mother (his father has recently died) leave the inn to get help in the next village but nobody there will do anything more than send a message to the authorities. Mrs Hawkins, knowing that she is unlikely to get Bones's unpaid rent if she does not take it herself, decides to return to the inn and search his room for the money. She takes Jim with her. They find plenty of money in the dead man's sea-chest but Mrs Hawkins insists on taking only what she is owed. As they are counting this out they hear the pirates returning. Hurriedly they take some of the money and Jim grabs a sealed packet to make up for the rest. They run outside and hide nearby, watching the pirates ransack the inn in a vain search for something. Then a mounted party of revenue officers arrives and the pirates run away, though they leave Blind Pew behind and in the confusion he is ridden down and killed.

Jim goes with the leader of the revenue men to the house of Squire John Trelawnay to deliver to him the sealed packet. He finds the squire with Dr Livesey. When they open the packet they find it contains a map of Treasure Island, with enough information for them to find the island and the pirate treasure of Captain Flint. The squire immediately decides to hire a ship and sail to the island. He asks Dr Livesey and Jim to go, too. The doctor urges secrecy and then the squire leaves for Bristol to find a ship. When Jim joins him there a few weeks later he finds that a schooner called the *Hispaniola* and a crew have been found, although it is plain that the squire has failed to keep quiet about the reason for the voyage. Soon after his arrival in Bristol Jim is sent with a message to the man hired as ship's cook, Long John Silver.

Jim's first meeting with Silver is at the tavern he runs near the docks. He is immediately taken with Silver's humour and vitality, and is so flattered that he persuades himself that, although Silver has only one leg, he is not the person Billy Bones feared. It becomes clear to the reader, however, that Silver is an expert in making himself agreeable to the squire and Jim and that he has had a strong influence on the choice of men for the crew of the *Hispaniola*. When Jim goes aboard with the squire and the doctor, he meets Alexander Smollett, the captain of the ship, who warns them that he does not like the reasons for their voyage or the look of the crew, but Squire Trelawnay refuses to listen and shows a dislike of Smollett that Jim shares.

They set sail, and Silver continues to enthral Jim with his talk. His influence over the rest of the crew, however, is striking, especially after the first mate, who should be in control, proves to be a drunkard and is eventually lost overboard. After an otherwise uneventful trip they near the island. With landfall imminent Jim goes on deck to get an apple from the open barrel there but, finding it nearly empty, has to climb inside. While hidden in the barrel he overhears Silver talking to one of the crew and persuading him to join the rest in a mutiny to gain the treasure. It is clear that Silver and his men have tricked the squire into taking them into his crew but that when the treasure is found they mean to kill the officers and take the gold for themselves.

Jim quickly alerts the squire, the doctor and the captain to

Silver's plot. They agree to do nothing to alert the pirates but
instead be on their guard. The island is sighted and it becomes
more and more obvious that the crew can hardly wait to get at the
treasure. When the ship anchors Captain Smollett announces
that the crew can go ashore and most of them, including Silver, do
so, leaving the ship to the squire, the doctor, the captain and a few
others. Jim, however, without telling the others, jumps into one of
the boats and also goes ashore, but as soon as he lands he runs off
into the trees that cover most of the island. As he is exploring it he
hears a terrible scream, which sounds like one of the men who has
refused to join the pirates has been murdered. He then overhears
Silver trying to persuade another loyal seaman to change sides
and, when he refuses, Jim witnesses his murder by Silver himself.
Fleeing for his life Jim encounters the island's only inhabitant,
Ben Gunn, who was marooned there some years before. The
solitude has nearly driven Gunn insane, but Jim promises him
that if he helps to defeat the pirates the squire will take him back
to England.

Meanwhile, as the doctor tells us in his narration, the men on
the ship decide to take what they can and abandon the *Hispaniola*
to the pirates. They load stores and weapons into one of the boats,
row ashore and take possession of the island's old stockade. When
the pirates realise this they open fire with one of the ship's cannon
but do no damage. Jim joins the others in the stockade and next
morning Silver appears with a flag of truce to offer terms, but
Captain Smollett rejects them, making Silver so angry he swears
to kill them all. The pirates then attack the stockade but are
beaten off with heavy losses, although Smollett, who has proved
to be an admirable leader, is severely wounded.

The doctor now goes to find Ben Gunn and, while nobody is
looking, Jim again runs off on his own. Gunn has told him that
there is a boat hidden on the shore and he at first goes to find it,
but then he notices that all but a couple of the pirates are on shore
and those still aboard the *Hispaniola* are not keeping a watch. He
decides to paddle out and cut the ship's anchor rope so that it
drifts ashore and the pirates cannot use it to escape. When he
does so, however, the falling tide pulls the *Hispaniola* out to sea,
along with the little boat containing Jim. He drifts all night and
next morning finds he cannot reach the shore because of the
currents. But he spots the ship drifting out of control and
manages to board her, where he finds the two pirates have fought
each other till one is dead and the other, Israel Hands, is
wounded, though able to tell Jim how to run the ship. They

manage to sail it round to the north end of the island and into an
inlet where they can beach it, but just as they are doing so Hands
suddenly jumps up and chases Jim with a knife. Jim escapes by
climbing the rigging. Hands follows but Jim shoots him with one
of the pistols he carries.

Jim is now the only person who knows where the ship is.
Pleased with himself he sets off to rejoin the others. It is dark
when he climbs into the stockade and he does not realise until too
late that it has been taken over by Silver and the other pirates.
His friends have not only disappeared but they have also handed
over the map to Silver. The other pirates, however, are in low
spirits and suspicious of Silver. They mutiny against him, but he
beats them down. Dr Livesey appears and Silver allows Jim to
talk to him alone, having made Jim swear not to try to escape.
Jim therefore refuses the doctor's suggestion that he climb out of
the stockade, but he tells him where he has left the *Hispaniola*.
Then he goes as a hostage with the pirates as they follow the map
in search of the treasure.

The map is not very clear but the pirates find the skeleton of
one of Flint's men laid out as a marker. This discovery unnerves
them and then they hear what sounds like a ghostly voice, which
frightens them even more. Silver, however, manages to talk them
out of their fears and they climb further inland until they find the
huge tree under which the treasure is buried. Jim and Silver hang
back as the others rush forward, only to find a large hole in the
ground. The treasure is gone. Instantly Long John Silver changes
sides again. He gives Jim a pistol and drawing his own confronts
the other pirates, who blame him for the disappointment. As they
attack, however, shots are fired from the trees. The doctor and
Ben Gunn (who had been trying to delay the pirates with his
ghostly singing so that the rescuers could get into position) have
arrived in time to rescue Jim and Silver. Two of the pirates are
killed and the remaining three run off.

Jim returns with the others to Ben Gunn's cave, where he finds
Gunn has piled up the treasure, which he found himself. Next day
they carry it down to the inlet and load it on to the *Hispaniola*.
Silver uses all his wiles to ingratiate himself with the people he
had been trying to kill shortly before and succeeds in being
allowed to join them on the ship. As they sail out of the inlet the
three surviving pirates call to them from the beach asking not to
be left behind but the *Hispaniola* carries on without them. They
manage to reach a port, where Silver escapes with a bag of gold,
but the others are glad to let him go and, having found some more

men to crew the ship, sail home to England with the bulk of the
treasure.

Characters

With one or possibly two exceptions, the characters in *Treasure
Island* are straightforward stereotypes. In contrast with the
twists and surprises of the plot, in characterisation (and also
setting) Stevenson largely gives readers what they expect. Thus,
the three leaders of the expedition are familiar types. Squire
Trelawnay is an English country gentleman, outspoken, honest, a
little dim and unable to imagine the world from anyone else's
perspective, and therefore both trusting and also impatient with
disagreement. He is the best shot in the party, no doubt because
his favourite pastime is hunting. He has a paternal care for his
servants but no doubt of his own social superiority and natural
right to act as leader. His inability to guard his tongue means that
Silver and the pirates soon learn that he has Flint's map and is
taking a ship to find the treasure.

   Dr Livesey, in contrast, is controlled and precise, with a clear
common sense which he expresses in direct and economical
speech. He is to some extent a curb on the squire's excesses,
though he never mistakes his social position so far as to presume
to tell Trelawnay what to do. As a medical man and an ex-soldier
he does his duty without question, and expects others to do the
same. He mediates between the squire and Captain Smollett, who
at first do not much like each other. The captain is not
enthusiastic enough about the voyage for the squire and he
expresses misgivings about the crew Trelawnay has chosen,
which calls in question the squire's judgement of character
(rightly so, as it soon turns out). For most of the voyage to the
island Smollett seems a reserved, even pedantic man, who does
little to make himself liked and who disapproves of the squire's
generosity to the crew. When the pirates attack, however, Captain
Smollett proves to be an inspiring and effective leader and it is
noticeable that he, rather than the squire, organises the defence
of the stockade and gives the orders. It is however to Trelawnay's
credit that he accepts this and does not try to interfere with
Smollett's commands. He has the sense to realise that the captain
is the best man for the job. The doctor also praises Smollett,
saying to Jim Hawkins in Chapter 19: 'That man Smollett... is a
better man than I am. And when I say that it means a deal, Jim.'

   On the other side, the pirate characters are equally conventional. Billy Bones is a complete version of the old sea-dog, with

his battered hat and clothes, his telescope, his sea-chest and his song 'Yo-ho-ho, and a bottle of rum!', introduced on the first page and echoing right through the novel. Bones sets the tone of the book with the mixture of fascination and horror that he evokes in Jim and the reader. As Jim says in the first chapter, the old captain, though frightening, was also 'a fine excitement in a quiet country life'. This mixture of the frightening and the exciting characterises the pirates throughout the novel. Both Black Dog and Blind Pew are fearsome characters but the jolt they give to the story sets it going. There is an ambivalence about the pirates, even after they have begun doing their worst on Treasure Island. Although they are dangerous criminals they are colourful characters who seem to have more vitality than their good opponents.

Ben Gunn, the character who stands between the pirates and the honest people, is also a type. His most obvious precursor is Robinson Crusoe, and in fact Stevenson made changes between the magazine and book versions of *Treasure Island* to reduce the similarities between his character and that of the hero of Daniel Defoe's famous novel of 1719. Originally, for example, Ben Gunn had, like Robinson Crusoe, dressed himself in goat skins, but Crusoe spends much longer on his desert island than Ben and it is more plausible that Ben still has the ragged remnants of his clothes. Stevenson makes him much more obviously affected by the solitude than Crusoe, who retains an amazing sanity despite his more lengthy isolation. Ben Gunn on the other hand strikes Jim, and the reader, as slightly crazy in his scattered speech and his obsession with things he has missed, such as toasted cheese. Where Defoe concentrates on the physical aspects of Crusoe's life on his island, Stevenson shows more insight into the mental torment Ben Gunn has undergone. His mental confusion, however, also serves the plot, because it explains his concealment of certain facts, notably the whereabouts of the treasure, until Stevenson is ready to reveal them.

The one character who is not a stereotype (although Stevenson's success has made him one) is Long John Silver. The sign of this is his unpredictability. Despite Billy Bones's warning about the man with one leg, we, like Jim Hawkins, can hardly believe that the talkative, laughing man whom we meet running the 'Spy-Glass' tavern is really a villain. He seems too jolly. Stevenson skilfully plays the reader along, dropping hints of Silver's piratical nature and then confusing us, as Silver confuses Jim, with another burst of his amusing talk. We do not expect a fierce pirate to be so skilful

with words. In the end Silver overreaches himself, although it is
only by accident that Jim hears the sea cook in Chapter 11 using
the same words which had won him over to persuade one of the
crew to join the mutiny. After that Jim and the reader can both
hear the double meanings in Silver's talk, the friendly tones and
bantering oaths which conceal deadly purposes.

Yet even after these purposes are in the open Long John is not
silenced. He goes on talking, often in attempts to alter the
perception of himself by describing his actions in alternative ways.
It is typical that before the pirates attack Silver should, in Chapter
20, first seek a parley with his enemies. A feature of his discussion
with Captain Smollett is the way he tries to say not only what he
himself wants but also what the captain must want, too, thus
attempting to direct the discussion along the lines Silver chooses
and towards the conclusion he desires. This happens in other
conversations. He is always putting words into people's mouths
and, through them, ideas into their minds. With Smollett this does
not work, since the captain is naturally a man careful with words,
who refuses to let Silver dictate the terms of the discussion, but
with the other pirates this is the secret of Silver's success, as in
Chapter 29, when he argues the crew out of mutiny against him.

He is not however just a talker. Unusually, he combines talk
with action, often shockingly, as in Chapter 14 when, his words
having failed to persuade Tom to join the pirates, he ends the
discussion by suddenly hurling his crutch at Tom and killing him.
The contrast between Silver's smooth tongue and his decisive use
of violence makes each more striking and adds to his
unpredictability, but that is increased by his ability to reason.
Unlike most of the other characters, including the other pirates,
Silver thinks for himself and as a result is shown to be able to
change his mind, since he can usually see more than one side to a
question and give himself a choice. This is what makes him such a
fascinating character in the last seven chapters of the novel, as
the plot converges on the climax of the search for the treasure.
Silver, knowing himself caught between his own pirates, who
distrust him, and the party of the squire and his friends, has to
work out where his best options lie in a situation which changes
rapidly and repeatedly. Jim records Silver's ingenuity in steering
a course to safety with something like admiration, as well as with
relief, for his own survival depends on Long John's success.

This brings us to the most problematic feature of Long John
Silver as a character: his moral status. He is, in plain terms, a liar,
a cheat, a thief and a murderer and yet he remains an attractive

rogue. Some of the reviewers of the novel when it was first published objected to the fact that Silver escapes punishment for his crimes at the end but most modern readers and critics seem to have no trouble accepting this, just as Trelawnay and Livesey are persuaded at least to tolerate their former enemy when he changes back to their side at the end. He becomes once more the humorous sea cook, always ready with a cheerful word, so that his villainy becomes forgotten. In a remarkable essay called 'The Persons of the Tale' (1895) Stevenson imagines Long John Silver and Captain Smollett arguing about their status in the novel. Silver wins by claiming that he is the author's favourite character:

> He does me fathoms better'n he does you — fathoms,
> he does. And he likes doing me. He keeps me on deck
> mostly all the time, crutch and all; and he leaves you
> measling in the hold, where nobody can't see you,
> nor wants to, and you may lay to that!

Given that Captain Smollett is near to being the bravest and most honest character in the book, is in a sense its moral centre, this praise of Silver is unsettling. Stevenson is acknowledging that moral excellence and literary excellence do not necessarily go together.

That leaves us with Jim Hawkins. He is in many ways a typical boy, which suits the story perfectly. He is eager and inquisitive, quick-witted and observant. As such he makes a good narrator. He can go where an adult might not without affecting what people do and say and he can express his feelings, and have things explained to him, in direct fashion. Whether he is anything more than a typical character depends on whether he grows up at all in the course of the story, and that in turn involves his relationship with the biggest influence on him, Long John Silver. Since the novel is mainly told from Jim's point of view, the narrative would seem to show the widening of his experience from his parental home in a quiet spot, via the city of Bristol, to the high seas and an exotic island. During the expedition Jim also learns more about other people and his own abilities. It is true that at home he seems to have quite a lot of personal responsibility, especially with the illness and death of his father, which leaves him to take a big share in the running of the 'Admiral Benbow'. On board ship he is at first a very minor figure but from the moment he overhears the pirates' plans his importance increases and he is emboldened to take initiatives. When the ship reaches the island he goes ashore without telling anybody. He negotiates with Ben Gunn as an equal. He again fails to ask permission when he leaves the stockade, leading on to his capture of the ship and beaching it in the north inlet, after successful single combat with Israel Hands. All this shows an increasing independence of mind and deed, suggesting that Jim is no longer just a boy, but perhaps the clearest sign that he has begun to grow up is his behaviour after he is captured by the pirates in Chapter 27. Although frightened, he speaks out and does not lose his nerve in dealing with the situation. More importantly, when the doctor asks him to break his word and escape, he declines, saying: 'you know right well you wouldn't do the thing yourself, neither you, nor squire, nor captain; and no more will I. Silver trusted me; I passed my word, and back I go' (Chapter 30). Here Jim ranks himself with adults and accepts responsibility for himself, rejecting Dr Livesey's offer to take the blame on his shoulders. At the same time Jim's narrative tells us that he has begun to understand what is going on between Silver and the other pirates; sometimes, indeed, more than they do. He is no longer a simple observer of what the grown-ups are playing at, and instead he becomes a real participant in the action, to whom in the end Silver himself will turn for support.

This however raises a problem, one that arises earlier in the book. When Jim boards the *Hispaniola* and takes command, with only the wounded Israel Hands for crew, the relationship that develops between them is a complex one in which both rely on and trust – and distrust – each other. There is a kind of equivalence between them and Jim seems more than half a pirate himself in this part of the book. On the other hand, he assumes a high moral tone with Hands, urging him to pray to God for forgiveness for his crimes, as though Jim as captain must see to the spiritual welfare of his crew. But Jim's relationship with Hands is only a shadow of his relationship with Long John Silver. It is Silver who acts as Jim's teacher, for example in Chapter 8, when they walk through Bristol docks together and Long John points out the ships and what is being done aboard them. At the crisis of the plot, when Jim is at the mercy of the pirates, it is Silver who protects him. He says that he sees himself in Jim, 'the picter of my own self when I was young and handsome' (Chapter 28), and that in turn sets us thinking that Jim has something of Long John about him. Jim's actions are the craftiest in the book after Silver's, whether by accident, as in the apple barrel incident, or through opportunism, when he steals the ship from the pirates, or by design, when he sneaks back to check what Israel Hands is up to. Jim's growing-up, then, looks uncomfortably like learning to imitate Long John Silver, the arch-villain of the story.

The character of Jim Hawkins is therefore like Long John Silver in hinting at the theme of Stevenson's later work, especially *The Strange Case of Dr Jekyll and Mr Hyde* (1886), that there is no hard and simple divide between good and evil in human nature. Though at this early stage of his writing Stevenson has not explicitly made this a theme of *Treasure Island*, it is possible to see in the equivocal status of Silver and the touches of selfishness in Jim Hawkins the beginnings at least of Stevenson's fascination with the mixed moral nature of his heroes.

Structure and Themes

A branch of modern literary theory tries to formulate the structure of heroic narratives in novels and films. Much of this work is based on Joseph Campbell's book *The Hero With a Thousand Faces* (1949), which argues that heroic tales from all ages and throughout the world have the same basic shape and contain a similar sequence of episodes. A convenient summary of Campbell's approach is provided by Christopher Vogler's *The Writer's Journey* (1992), which applies the Campbell template to a number of modern narratives, mainly films. The sequence of narrative events Vogler uses is as follows:

1. Heroes are introduced in the ORDINARY WORLD, where
2. they receive the CALL TO ADVENTURE.
3. They are RELUCTANT at first or REFUSE THE CALL, but
4. are encouraged by a MENTOR to
5. CROSS THE FIRST THRESHOLD and enter the Special World, where
6. they encounter TESTS, ALLIES, AND ENEMIES.
7. They APPROACH THE INMOST CAVE, crossing a second threshold
8. where they endure the ORDEAL.
9. They take possession of their REWARD and
10. are pursued on THE ROAD BACK to the Ordinary World.
11. They cross the third threshold, experience a RESURRECTION, and are transformed by the experience.
12. They RETURN WITH THE ELIXIR, a boon or treasure to benefit the Ordinary World.

It is not difficult to discern something like this pattern of events in many adventure films. George Lucas, the maker of the *Star Wars* films, is said to have been influenced by Campbell's theory. It is weakened by Vogler's admission that the stages of the scheme 'can

be deleted, added to, and drastically shuffled without losing any of
their power' (p. 26). Nevertheless, it is illuminating to apply this
narrative template to *Treasure Island*, not only to see how far
Stevenson's novel conforms to the pattern but also to find out
where it differs.

It is obvious that *Treasure Island* begins in the Ordinary World.
The quiet little inn which is Jim Hawkins's home and the setting of
the opening chapters sets up a normal starting-point for the story.
We begin in rural England, with a squire as head of society and a
doctor for the welfare of its members. Social order is maintained by
recognised authority, present in the novel in the shape of the
revenue men. Into this world, however, comes the pirate Billy
Bones, followed by others. They will sound the Call to Adventure,
first in a general way, by the prospect the old sea-dog opens up of a
different world beyond the 'Admiral Benbow', and then very
specifically by means of the map of Treasure Island, which offers a
direct opening from the Ordinary World to the Special World.

Here we meet the first problem with the application of the
narrative scheme to *Treasure Island*. It cannot really be said that
the hero is reluctant to respond to the Call to Adventure, and he
certainly does not refuse it. Perhaps this is because of his youth.
On the one hand, Jim is too young to know what he may be letting
himself in for by taking up the challenge of the treasure map; on
the other hand, he is so young the decision is really taken for him
by Squire Trelawnay and Dr Livesey. It is striking that at the end
of Chapter 6, when the map has been revealed and Trelawnay and
Livesey rapidly decide to go in search of the treasure, Jim says not
a word. It is the doctor who speaks for him.

Does that therefore make the doctor, or the squire, the Mentor
figure the narrative template includes? 'The function of Mentors,'
says Vogler, 'is to prepare the hero to face the unknown. They may
give advice, guidance or magical equipment' (p. 18). The examples
he gives are Merlin in the tales of King Arthur or Obi-Wan Kenobi
in the earliest *Star Wars* film. Jim Hawkins could certainly do
with such a friend at the beginning of *Treasure Island* but it is not
clear that he has one. As in *Kidnapped*, where however the theme
is more developed, the hero of the novel more or less begins it
without a father-figure (Jim's father is a shadowy character who
dies in Chapter 3) and the novel is partly about his quest for
someone to guide him. Dr Livesey and Squire Trelawnay are the
most obvious candidates but, as we have seen, they take Jim
rather for granted. The squire is in any case not really much more
mature than Jim, for all that he is older, and the boy's

relationship with the doctor is curiously restrained. So also is his relationship with the third adult leader of the expedition, Captain Smollett. Vogler's scheme has the merit of drawing attention to the way Stevenson distances his hero from the conventional leaders of his society, which leaves us to consider some unconventional possibilities as his Mentor.

The first is Billy Bones, who does indeed give Jim advice and guidance, and in a sense he also gives Jim the extraordinary object, the map, which will enable him to enter the world of adventure. It is Bones, with his stories and songs, who tells Jim about this world, and he it is who warns him against the one-legged seaman (if there is any hint of reluctance to enter the Special World in Jim's case, it comes in the form of his nightmares about the one-legged man). But if Billy Bones fulfils some part of the role of Mentor to Jim, he does so in a limited and doubtful way. A much more significant though still unconventional Mentor is Long John Silver. He is the man who dominates Jim's preparations for the voyage and the period up to the arrival at the island. It is his advice and guidance we hear much of, not that of Trelawnay, Livesey and Smollett. Silver is presented as the expert on ships, sailing, pirates and the island itself, and we are left in no doubt that it is to him that Jim listens most during the approach to Treasure Island. The narrative scheme, then, again points to an unusual feature of Stevenson's novel and reinforces the suggestion already made above that there is a relationship between Jim Hawkins and Long John Silver that cuts across moral conventions. It also suggests the complexity of Silver's role in the plot, in which he acts as both the main friend of the hero and his chief enemy.

The next phase of the narrative scheme is the crossing of the threshold into the Special World. This can surely be identified in *Treasure Island* with the arrival at the island itself. Stevenson adds to the significance of this moment in the plot by making it almost coincide with Jim's discovery of Silver's treachery and the pirates' plot, the trigger for which is assumed to be the landing on the island, and the sense of reaching a crucial point in the narrative is also marked by Jim's sudden break away from the others when he goes ashore himself. For almost the first time in the novel, and certainly the first time since discovering the map, Jim is alone and, however unwisely, acting independently.

Now begins the period of tests, allies and enemies. While exploring the island, Jim finds himself close enough to witness Silver's murder of the loyal seaman Tom. Jim's reaction is intense: 'the whole world swam away from before me in a whirling mist'

and he almost faints. When he recovers, and realises his danger,
he is filled with fear that turns 'into a kind of frenzy' (Chapter 14).
Nevertheless, he passes the test of courage and runs away, to
encounter an ally, Ben Gunn, from whom he learns much. Jim has
now become a major player in the plot and has the confidence to
go on influencing events. When he rejoins the others in the
stockade he will face the further test of the attack of the pirates
and take an active part in defeating them, snatching up a cutlass
to sally out with the others at the crisis of the battle.

According to the narrative scheme of the Campbell/Vogler
theory, all this should culminate in a particularly dangerous
episode in which the hero risks extreme danger to win the highest
prize (points 7 and 8 in the list above), but there seems to be no
'inmost cave' for the hero to enter. Where is the moment of ordeal
in *Treasure Island*? It seems to consist of the whole sequence of
events after the battle, when Jim again goes off on his own, at
first to find Ben Gunn's boat, and then to use it to cut loose the
schooner, which he will later board and sail to a secret location.
There is certainly an element of ordeal about this. When the tide
whirls him out to sea at the end of Chapter 23 Jim fears that he
will soon be drowned and lies down in the boat to await his fate: 'a
numbness, an occasional stupor, fell upon my mind,' he says.
Chapter 24 begins with Jim still in danger and almost at the
mercy of the sea but gradually he masters the situation and in the
end it brings him to the ship and the triumph of his capture of it.
He certainly may be said to have crossed a threshold when he
goes aboard and pronounces himself its captain, though he has to
prove himself by defeating Israel Hands. Once Hands is dead and
the *Hispaniola* is beached in the North Inlet, Jim is left as the
only person who knows where it is and so he now controls the
destiny of everybody else on the island at a moment when none of
them know where he is or if he is still alive. His knowledge of the
whereabouts of the ship opens the road home. Having captured
the ship Jim has not only secured a great reward for his actions
but also taken the first step of his and the other characters' return
to the ordinary world.

Before that, however, another complex series of events
intervenes. Jim is not really being pursued here, as the narrative
scheme specifies, but his return is impeded and he must overcome
life-threatening dangers. When in the darkness Jim crosses
another threshold and enters the stockade he blunders straight
into the pirates' lair. Here he faces a trial at least as perilous as
that in the small boat and on the schooner. Perhaps it is worse

because it requires not just physical bravery but also quick-wittedness and a kind of moral courage. By luck and good management Jim stays in control of the situation in his sea adventure but as a prisoner of the pirates he is much less able to control his own fate and has to learn to bide his time and wait for the right moment to save himself. There is a different sort of heroism involved here and the whole episode is darker (literally so in the stockade in Chapter 28) and more threatening. Jim is a hostage and led like a sacrificial victim. At the climax he will find himself facing deadly enemies on the edge of a grave-like pit, to which a skeleton has pointed the way. His survival may almost be likened to a resurrection and the whole episode surely transforms him. As already noted, Jim grows in moral stature when he rejects the Doctor's suggestion that he break his word and instead stands by his promise to Silver.

The novel therefore does seems to conform to the sequence of events listed as items seven to eleven by Vogler. Where there is a real puzzle, however, is in the nature of his reward. What is it that Jim brings back to the Ordinary World? Of course this is supposed to be what is stated in the title of the novel – treasure – but as W. W. Robson asks, in his essay 'The Sea Cook: A Study in the Art of Robert Louis Stevenson' (one of the best critical studies of *Treasure Island*), 'why does the *treasure* count so little, emotionally, in the tale?' Stevenson pulls off his trick on the pirates, and the first-time reader, by making the finding of the treasure-site an anti-climax; and the sense of disappointment continues beyond into the close of the novel. Chapter 34 includes just a paragraph describing the treasure, principally the coins it includes, but we are probably more struck by the toil of carrying the gold down to the ship. After that little is said about it. Long John Silver steals a bag, but the only person who to our knowledge spends any of the money is Ben Gunn, who in nineteen days squanders a thousand pounds, a huge sum in those days. It is not clear what use Jim makes of his share.

Thus there seems no equivalent in *Treasure Island* to the elixir or boon that the Campbell/Vogler scheme says the hero returns with to the Ordinary World. This may lead us to ask what exactly is the final reward for the hero of the novel. We have seen that Stevenson seems to provide two different ordeals for Jim, from one of which he returns with the ship and from the second of which he returns empty-handed, because the treasure has already been found. Jim has been looking in the wrong place for it and perhaps the reader also looks in the wrong place if he or she thinks the hero's reward is simply material wealth. Stevenson, having offered us a conventional tale of a treasure hunt and satisfied our liking for pirates and adventure on a tropical island, at the end draws back from the conventional a little and leaves us to wonder what the story was really about.

The narrative pattern based on the theories of Campbell and Vogler does not completely fit *Treasure Island* but it does illuminate some aspects of the general shape of the novel. Oddly, it is perhaps most useful where it does not fit because that draws attention to significant features of the book and raises questions about its meaning. Stevenson of course had absolutely no knowledge of this narrative theory and it would be quite wrong to say that where his novel does not conform to it he somehow failed to get it right. What is striking is that *Treasure Island* should have so much in common with this modern idea of what makes a good narrative. We might take that as a measure of Stevenson's genius. Although this book has not space to do so, the scheme can also be applied to *Kidnapped*, but again its value may be in showing us where Stevenson's plotting is different from the Campbell/Vogler pattern. It applies much less well to *Catriona*, which may be an indication that that is a different kind of novel from the other two.

Kidnapped

Stevenson began writing *Kidnapped* in March 1885 and completed it the following year. Although he had found the beginning and middle of the novel easy to write, he only finished it after a friend suggested that, instead of trying to bring the whole story to a conclusion, he should leave some things unresolved at the end and promise there would be a sequel. *Kidnapped* first appeared as a serial in the magazine *Young Folks* before publication as a book. It was immediately successful with both readers and critics and, after the success of *Dr Jekyll and Mr Hyde* earlier in 1886, it confirmed Stevenson's arrival as an author and at last gave him the prospect of steady income from his writings.

Historical Background

The novel is set in 1751, about five years after the defeat of the last Jacobite Rebellion. The origins of this event lie in the previous century. In 1688 the ruling member of the Stewart dynasty, King James VII (of Scotland) and II (of England), was forced off the throne of the United Kingdom of England, Scotland and Ireland by the English Parliament because of his religion. As a Roman Catholic he was suspected of favouring the influence of England's traditional enemy, France, and of wishing to reverse the break-away of the Church of England from the Roman Catholic church. James was replaced as monarch by his daughter Mary, who ruled jointly with her husband, the Dutchman William of Orange. James's supporters, known as Jacobites after the Latin form, Jacobus, of his name, rose in rebellion in Scotland and Ireland but were defeated. James went into exile in France, where he continued to hope for a return to power in Britain.

William and Mary were succeeded by Mary's sister, Anne, but she was childless and so, in order to maintain a Protestant succession, the English Parliament arranged for the throne to pass to the Elector of Hanover in Germany. To ensure that Scotland accepted this the English offered and secured the Union of the Parliaments of England and Scotland in 1707. Nevertheless, when Anne died and the Elector took the throne as George I, there was another Jacobite rebellion in 1715, mainly in the Highlands, in the name of the son of James VII and II, also called James, and known to the Jacobites as James VIII and III. This rebellion too was unsuccessful but dissatisfaction with the Hanoverians as rulers and, in Scotland, a dislike of the union with England kept Jacobite feeling alive, especially among the Highland clans, who, unlike the

Scottish Lowlanders, remained Roman Catholics like the exiled
Stewarts.

In 1745 Charles Edward Stewart, the son of James VIII and III,
landed on the west coast of Scotland. Because of his youth and
good looks Charles was known as Bonnie Prince Charlie. Despite
the fact that he arrived with only a handful of followers and no
more than promises of military support from France, then at war
with Britain, Charles soon gathered an army of Highlanders and
after skilful and rapid marching Edinburgh, the capital of
Scotland, was seized and the Jacobites defeated a government
army at Prestonpans, just east of the city.

The Jacobite army now advanced into England, causing panic
in London. But when the Highlanders reached Derby they
hesitated and turned back. The clans felt vulnerable so far from
their mountains and the hoped-for support from English Jacobites
had not emerged. Pursued by government forces the rebels
returned to Scotland and, although they were again victorious in
battle at Falkirk, in the centre of the Lowlands, they retreated
into the Highlands. In April 1746 a strong government force
commanded by the Duke of Cumberland brought the Jacobites to
battle at Culloden outside Inverness and routed them.

Cumberland's troops went on to harry the territories of the
Jacobite clans, killing and burning, and imposing a harsh rule on
the Highlands designed to break the power of the clans for ever.
Laws were passed to end the powers of the clan chiefs and to
prohibit the symbols of clan rule, such as wearing tartan and
playing bagpipes. The result was a devastating blow to the culture
and economy of the Highlands, bringing about a growing volume
of emigration, forced and voluntary, as the people of the
Highlands left to seek new lives elsewhere, some in the Lowland
cities of Scotland, such as Glasgow, but many overseas, in
America, Australia and New Zealand.

Jacobite chiefs were imprisoned and executed, or driven, like
Prince Charles himself, into exile, mainly in France. Their lands
were seized by the British crown. Not all the clans were Jacobites,
however. One of the largest, the Clan Campbell, led by its chief, the
Duke of Argyle, fought on the Hanoverian side. The Campbells
became the dominant clan in the Highlands, hated and feared by
their defeated enemies. It is into this situation that David Balfour,
the hero of *Kidnapped*, comes. He, as a Lowland Scot and a
Protestant, has little knowledge of the clan rivalries in the
Highlands and, like most Lowlanders of his time, thinks the defeat
of the Jacobite Rebellion was a restoration of peace and order.

Outline

Kidnapped begins with its hero and narrator David Balfour taking leave of his native village after the death of his father (his mother has died some years before). He is accompanied to the edge of Essendean by the local minister, Mr Campbell, who gives David advice and a letter left by his father and addressed to David's uncle, Ebenezer Balfour, of the House of Shaws at Cramond, near Edinburgh. This is the first David has heard of his uncle and he sets out to visit him full of pleasant visions of being the nephew of a wealthy landowner, but when he reaches Cramond and asks for the House of Shaws he soon detects that his uncle is not popular with his neighbours.

Night has fallen when David at last approaches his uncle's house, which he finds run-down and almost in darkness. After some difficulty he manages to persuade his uncle to admit him and finds that Ebenezer is a thorough miser, living in darkness and squalor, and not at all happy to meet his nephew. David begins to suspect that there is a family secret Ebenezer is hiding, and that in fact David's father should have inherited the House of Shaws, which would make David now the rightful owner. He suspects Ebenezer would be glad to get rid of him.

One night these suspicions are confirmed. Ebenezer persuades David to climb up a half-finished tower in the dark and only luck prevents him from falling to his death from the broken staircase. But next morning, before David can settle matters with his uncle, a young lad called Ransome arrives with a message from Captain Hoseason, of the trading brig *Covenant*, with whom Ebenezer has business dealings. David, who is anxious to see the ships and the sea, agrees to go with Ebenezer and Ransome to meet Hoseason at Queensferry. There he is so interested in the sailors and the ships that he allows his uncle and the captain to discuss their business without him. He is so impressed by Hoseason (another of Stevenson's two-faced characters) that he is persuaded to go aboard the brig, where he is promptly knocked on the head. He wakes up to find himself tied up below decks, kidnapped.

The *Covenant* sails down the Firth of Forth. David is visited by one of the officers, Mr Riach, who tends the bump on his head and lets him know they are bound for America, where David will be sold as a slave. It soon becomes clear that, in the dark and dirty hold, David is becoming more and more unwell. Riach, who is on the whole not a bad man, persuades Hoseason that David should be moved to a bed in the crew's quarters in the forecastle. There he slowly recovers and learns more about the ship and those

aboard. The *Covenant* is attempting to sail around the north of
Scotland and into the Atlantic but the winds are adverse and she
makes little progress, which frustrates and irritates her officers
and crew.

The boy Ransome is the officers' servant, living apart from the
rest of the crew in the roundhouse further aft, where he supplies
the captain, Riach and the first mate Shuan with their meals and,
more importantly, their drink. Mr Shuan in particular is an ill-
tempered, violent drunkard, although he is also the best seaman
on board. One day he lashes out at Ransome, mortally injuring
him. Hoseason makes David take his place.

They have now rounded the north of Scotland but give up the
attempt to sail directly west and instead turn south through the
Hebrides, the western isles. The ship runs into dense fog and
collides with a small boat, out of which there is only one survivor,
who is quick and agile enough to jump up and grab a hold on the
Covenant before his boat sinks. The newcomer is Alan Breck
Stewart, a striking figure in a French military uniform. More
interesting to Hoseason and his men is the fact that Alan Breck is
carrying a large quantity of gold. He is in fact a Jacobite courier
who is taking back to France the money he has collected from his
fellow-clansmen to support their exiled chief.

Alan Breck is forced to offer Hoseason a large payment to be
landed back on the coast of Scotland, but not in territory
controlled by his enemies the Campbells. Hoseason agrees and
leaves Alan Breck in the roundhouse to be served a meal by
David. When he asks for a drink, David goes to find the captain to
ask for the key to the liquor store and overhears the officers
plotting to attack the Jacobite and take his gold. David pretends
to join in but when he returns to the roundhouse he warns Alan of
his danger and agrees to take his side.

Fortunately the roundhouse is where all the firearms in the
ship are kept. David loads several pistols while Alan draws his
sword and prepares to defend the only open door. It is not long
before the crew attack. Shuan is killed by Alan and David,
guarding the windows behind him, fires several shots and wounds
the captain. After a lull there is another, more determined assault
but Alan and David beat it off, killing and wounding several more
of the crew. Hoseason is forced to call a truce and negotiate terms
with Alan, who still insists on being put ashore. The captain has
to agree but admits that he now has hardly enough men left to
sail the ship.

Alan is highly delighted with the victory and full of praise for

David's part in it. He gives him a silver button from his coat as a token of friendship. For his part, David finds himself more and more attracted to his new friend, despite the fact that in politics, religion and moral outlook they are quite opposite. It is from Alan that he now learns about the consequences of the Jacobite Rebellion for the Highlands and, in particular, how Colin Campbell, known as the Red Fox, has been trying to drive the Stewarts of Appin from their land so that he and the Campbells can take it over.

The fog has lifted and the ship sails briskly south through the islands but, with the death of Shuan, the only man who knew these waters, nobody on board is quite sure where they are. When night falls Hoseason appeals for help to Alan, who has often sailed to and from the coast thereabouts. He comes on deck and suggests that they are near the Isle of Mull and that to avoid the reefs they should sail close in to the island. Nevertheless, the *Covenant* strikes the rocks and is wrecked. As he helps in the struggle to launch the ship's boat David is washed overboard. He is carried away from the ship and, clinging to a spar, drifts to land on what he thinks is a small, barren island.

For several days David, wet and cold, survives on shell-fish, which sometimes make him sick, feeling totally lost and abandoned. One day he sees a boat passing and implores the occupants for rescue but they only laugh at him. Next day, however, the same boat returns. There is another man in it who tries to speak to David but his English is so bad the lad has great difficulty understanding what he says. Then suddenly he makes out the word 'tide' and realises that the island is not cut off when the tide is low. By pure bad luck David has never been on the landward side at low tide but as soon as he goes there he discovers that it is quite easy to wade over to Mull itself. Feeling a fool he makes for the house whose chimney smoke he had watched from the 'island' and there he finds food and shelter and the news that several other survivors came ashore from the wreck. Among them was Alan, who has left word that David should follow him to Appin.

David sets out across the Isle of Mull and then through Morven, meeting a variety of people on the way. Despite the fact that he does not speak Gaelic he copes, with the aid of the silver button, which brings him the help of Alan's friends. From the ferry that he takes to cross from Mull to the mainland he sees a large ship bound for America laden with emigrants and is moved by their sad farewell to the people they leave behind. As he nears his destination he meets a troop of soldiers led by a man on a horse. He stops the man and asks for directions to the house of Alan's kinsman, James of the Glens, but David has in fact met the Red Fox, Colin Campbell, on his way to evict the Appin Stewarts.

While David is talking to Campbell a shot is fired from the hill behind them and the Red Fox falls from his horse, fatally wounded. David turns and sees what he thinks is the murderer running over the hill and goes off in pursuit, but is surprised to hear one of Campbell's companions ordering the soldiers to fire at him, as an accomplice who kept the Red Fox talking so that the assassin could shoot him. David himself now runs for his life but when he reaches the trees further up the slope is surprised to meet Alan Breck, standing alone with a fishing rod in his hand. Stifling argument Alan leads David away from the scene, but he notices that every so often Alan allows them to be spotted by the soldiers, who are thus drawn away from the path taken by the murderer. After a while, however, Alan doubles back and they sneak past the soldiers to return, this time unseen, to the wood from which they started.

David begins by accusing Alan of the shooting but Alan rejects this. He does not deny, however, that he wanted the Red Fox dead and has no wish to help the Campbells find his killer. David is all for giving themselves up to clear themselves of the accusation of involvement in the killing but Alan rejects this too. He has no doubt that they would be tried and condemned by a court full of Campbells out for revenge. Instead they must flee the Highlands but since they have no money he says they must go and borrow some from James of the Glens. When they reach his house they find it in turmoil. James expects to be arrested at any moment and his followers are frantically hiding weapons and burning documents. He tells Alan and David that for his own sake he must send out wanted notices describing them as the murderers but he also provides them with money and other necessaries and they set off into the night.

Now begins the most exciting and memorable section of the novel, several chapters with the general heading of 'The Flight in the Heather' in which David and Alan flee across the moors and mountains, in good weather and bad, chased by soldiers and encountering a variety of people, friend and foe, high and low. In the course of this journey their friendship is severely tested and David's health suffers so badly that he is hardly able to go on. At last they reach the Lowlands but find that they cannot cross the River Forth at Stirling because the bridge there, the last before the river broadens into the Firth of Forth, is guarded against them. They carry on down the north bank rather aimlessly until they come to Limekilns in Fife, from where they can see across the water to Queensferry, where David was kidnapped. They go into a public house to buy some food and are served by a pretty girl. This gives Alan an idea. He makes David act as though he is too exhausted to continue and plays on the girl's sympathy so that she offers to help them across the Forth. David and Alan wait in a nearby wood until nightfall and then the girl rows them across to the southern shore in a boat she has stolen.

Next day David, leaving Alan hiding outside Queensferry, goes into the town in search of Mr Rankeillor, a lawyer whose name he remembers from his time with his uncle. Despite his ragged appearance, David succeeds in gaining an interview with Rankeillor, to whom he reveals his identity and his claims against his uncle. Fortunately the lawyer, as well as being a fair-minded man, has also formed his own suspicions of Ebenezer. He is able to tell David more of his family history. It seems that David's father and his brother Ebenezer both fell in love with the same woman and, after much argument, agreed that Ebenezer should have the estate of Shaws while David's father should marry the woman, who thus became David's mother.

Rankeillor is willing to help David but on one point he is very cautious. He wants to avoid knowing anything about such a notorious Jacobite as Alan Breck and insists that David refer to him only as 'Mr Thomson', so that he can honestly say he has never heard of the Highlander. With this proviso he agrees to meet Alan and arrange a plan to trap Ebenezer into admitting his guilt. Accompanied by his clerk Rankeillor goes with David, to whom he has given a decent suit of clothes, to meet Alan as evening falls. They then all go to the House of Shaws. With the others in hiding, Alan calls Ebenezer out of the house and, pretending that he has David prisoner and has come to negotiate a ransom, skilfully leads the old man to admit his complicity in the kidnapping. At that David, Rankeillor and his clerk step forward. They all go into the house and the lawyer makes Ebenezer sign an agreement to pay David two-thirds of the income from the estate.

Next morning David and Alan set out for Edinburgh. David is determined that he will try to give evidence in the case of the Appin Murder, despite the danger to himself, but he will also make arrangements for Alan's escape to France. After a reluctant farewell he leaves Alan outside the city and makes his way to the bank to collect some of the money due to him.

Characters

Kidnapped takes the form of a narrative about the growth to adulthood of its leading character, David Balfour, and is therefore what is called a *Bildungsroman*, a German word meaning a novel about growing up. This makes it like a number of other novels in English such as Charles Dickens's *Great Expectations* (1861) and D H Lawrence's *Sons and Lovers* (1913). David is a typical young man about to start on life. He has seen little of the world and in dealing with people relies on limited experience and what he has been taught by his parents and teachers. The narrowness of his education is made clear to us in the first chapter when he takes his leave of Mr Campbell, whose advice and gifts are well-meant but almost comically inadequate. The fact, however, that David himself is amused by the recipe 'To Make Lilly of the Valley Water' at least shows us that he has common sense and intelligence, which he is going to need if he is to survive and prosper.

Yet David is too young to do this alone and he seems to realise this in the way that he repeatedly tries to attach himself to somebody older and wiser to guide him. In a way the story can be seen as consisting of David's quest for a substitute for the father who has died before it begins and whose death causes David's entry into the wider world. Certainly the opening of the novel is driven by David's search for a father-figure. Mr Campbell proves inadequate as well as unwilling; there seems to be no question of David's staying in Essendean with him. He sets off for his uncle's in high hopes of finding a replacement for his father there but is soon disappointed. This does not stop him next trusting in Hoseason, to his cost again, and then in Mr Riach. In the end his tendency to link up with an older man will lead him to join with Alan Breck and at last find someone he can rely on, though this does not stop him from appealing to Cluny Macpherson as a son to a father in Chapter 23 and taking up a filial attitude again when he meets Mr Rankeillor at the end of the novel. A basic rhythm of the plot of *Kidnapped* is the repeated encounters between the hero and a series of older men.

When David first introduces himself to Alan in Chapter 9 he admits to being 'betwixt and between'. This indicates his unformed state of mind and character. There is much he is undecided about, and he shows himself slow to reach conclusions. He does however have some definite principles, although he is awkward about applying them, as the quarrel with Alan over the card-playing at Cluny's Cage shows. He is on the whole a supporter of the Protestant King George, which makes him what

Alan calls a Whig in religion and politics, and he would like to believe in the integrity of the legal system of his country. He believes in justice and in telling the truth, even at his own peril, but although he is shocked by Alan's Highland interpretation of both of these David is not so moralistic as to turn against his friend for this reason. In the end, he shows a very modern tolerance for alternative ideas to his own, provided his are in turn respected. This makes him a bit of an anachronism for his period, rather as though Stevenson has sent a lad of his own time and temperament back a hundred years, but it also makes David a useful means of introducing the reader to the events and attitudes of the time of the novel. David's ignorance about the Highlands, for example, justifies Stevenson in making Alan teach him, and through him the reader, all about the clans.

So far only one of the David Balfours in the novel has been described. There is a second: not David Balfour the character but David Balfour the narrator. He is a shadowy figure. We assume from his tone of voice that he is much older than the David whose story is being told. The narrator often comments on his earlier self's ignorance or naivety, as though he has now learnt better. But exactly what has become of David between the events of *Kidnapped* and his writing them down is not clear (some answers will be given in the sequel, *Catriona*). It seems in *Kidnapped* as if Stevenson has not really thought about David's later life yet. Perhaps this was because when he wrote the novel he himself, despite being much older than David the character, had little direct experience of adult responsibilities. Stevenson was still dependent on his father and was only just beginning to have the success as a writer which would allow him to make a full career as an author.

The other main character in the novel is Alan Breck. He is the most attractive and exciting character in the novel and as soon as he enters it the tempo of the story increases. As mentioned above, he acts as David's mentor, leading him both physically and mentally into and through the Highlands, teaching David much about people and places and about himself as they go. Though David would no doubt like to lean on Alan as a father-figure, Alan himself is often too unconventional to be an adult role-model. He is sometimes more like an elder brother than a father, as when he and David compete at 'guddling' trout in Chapter 21. At other times Alan forces David to do things and thus makes him take responsibility for himself. A very typical and climactic example of this is in Chapter 20 when they must jump across a river in spate and Alan almost cruelly drives David into leaping across the roaring water.

Alan makes David take responsibility for himself by not doing everything for him and by treating him as an equal, if not in knowledge then in basic ability. When they meet people Alan insists on their treating David as his friend and when they are alone and making plans Alan listens to what David has to say, even if he disagrees. He then explains what to do fully and fairly. This is not to say that Alan does not have his faults. He is quick-tempered and vain, especially about his name and his appearance. David thinks Alan's personal vanity is rather unmanly. Alan can also be petulant and sulk when he feels slighted or in the wrong, but not only do these faults make him seem human they in some ways also enhance his virtues of courage and loyalty, because he quickly gets over his bad moods. Even the big quarrel between Alan and David in Chapter 24 adds to our admiration for Alan because its outcome shows Alan readily forgiving and forgetting what David has said and blaming himself for the argument. A similar good impression is made in the piping contest with Robin Oig Macgregor in the next chapter, when, despite his initial boasting, in the end Alan generously concedes that Robin is a much better player.

Like Long John Silver, Alan Breck is a character with an eloquent voice. Although his language is not so full of personality as Long John's it is still the most distinctive in the novel. He is rarely lost for words and he fills his talk with jokes, references to people he knows, snatches of proverbs and songs and surprising turns of phrase. It is of course his place in the novel to be a source of information and experience and this gives him a position of authority and control that adds to his stature and makes what he says interesting to the reader, but Stevenson never allows him to become preachy or dull. Partly this is because of the way Stevenson constructs the dialogues between Alan and David, exploiting the possibilities of having two main characters. David's interruptions and questions when Alan is speaking are often sharp and provocative so that he is never a passive listener.

All the other characters in *Kidnapped* are minor ones who appear only once, with one exception. That is David's uncle Ebenezer Balfour, whose appearances at the beginning and end of the story frame it and give it shape. Ebenezer is a stereotypical greedy miser, a man who will deny even himself the comforts of warmth, light and food. No doubt he gets his name from Ebenezer Scrooge, the main character in Charles Dickens's fable *A*

Christmas Carol (1843), although unlike Scrooge David's uncle never reforms and learns charity. Like all the other minor characters, and even Alan Breck, Ebenezer does not change in the course of the novel (indeed, it is a matter for debate whether David himself develops as a character, although he does learn more about the world and himself).

Stevenson fills the novel with a great range of characters, of all ages, from the ship's boy Ransome to the old man on Mull who first sees David after he lands there, and all classes, from the blind catechist in Chapter 25 to Colin Campbell, the Red Fox, in Chapter 27. We meet seamen such as Hoseason and Riach, a Highland chief in Cluny Macpherson and Mr Rankeillor, the Scots lawyer. Not only does Stevenson gives us economical and memorable descriptions of each of these characters when they appear but he also makes them speak in different but appropriate ways. Mr Rankeillor's Latin tags show his Classical learning just as the nautical characters' language shows their professional concerns. Cluny Macpherson's courtly politeness is combined with an insistence on his own wishes that conveys his autocratic self-importance. As in *Treasure Island*, Stevenson is skilful in establishing what characters are like as soon as they open their mouths.

Amongst the crowd of characters in *Kidnapped* there is however one group that seems under-represented. There are very few women in the novel and only three have speaking parts. Two of these are brief. Jennet Clouston appears for only a couple of paragraphs in Chapter 2 to curse Ebenezer and the House of Shaws, and in Chapter 19 the wife of James of the Glens has one short speech in which she blesses David for agreeing to help her husband. A more substantial part in the action is played by the girl in the change house at Limekilns, who is persuaded to find Alan and David a boat to cross the Forth, and in fact rows them over herself. Remarkably, Stevenson does not even give her a name, although in *Catriona*, the sequel to *Kidnapped*, he not only tells us she is called Alison Hastie but first that David sent her a present for helping Alan and him and then, right at the end of the novel, we learn that he even employed her as a servant. It seems Stevenson was trying to make amends for neglecting this character in the first novel but in doing so he surely makes things worse, for how could David have forgotten to mention her name if she had actually joined his household when he settled down after his adventures?

This is symptomatic of the wider problem of Stevenson's treatment of female characters. He was aware that in his early fiction he did not deal with these very well and therefore often avoided using them. He admitted in a note on one of his other novels, *The Master of Ballantrae* (1889), that 'I am always afraid of my women, who are not admired in my home circle', showing that he was nervous about creating female characters and about the criticism they attracted. It is noticeable that he virtually omits them in *Treasure Island*, where the only woman is Jim's mother and she is left behind after a few chapters. Undoubtedly, having put very few women into *Kidnapped*, Stevenson set out to use more in the sequel, centring it on Catriona and including two other notable female characters. Whether this succeeds in redressing the balance is however still debatable.

Structure and Themes
Kidnapped is a Scottish historical novel in the tradition established by Sir Walter Scott, whose works Stevenson knew well. Scott's first novel, *Waverley* (1814), sets a pattern in plot, setting and characterisation which Stevenson follows in *Kidnapped*. In Scott's novel the hero, Edward Waverley, is a young man starting out in life who travels north into the Highlands. There he meets a Highland chief, Fergus MacIvor, and is so enthralled by him that he actually joins the Jacobite army in the 1745 Rebellion as it captures Edinburgh, wins the Battle of Prestonpans and invades England. In the retreat back to Scotland, however, Waverley is separated from the Highlanders and, thanks to influential friends, escapes punishment when the rebellion is defeated. He is able to settle down to a more normal life as a country landowner, having married the daughter of one of the Jacobites.

The plot of *Kidnapped* has much the same shape, with the movement of David Balfour into the Highlands and his journey through them and back to near his starting-point, but with an elevation of his social situation and prospects at the end. On the journey David, like Waverley, comes under the influence of a charismatic Highlander and not only learns about the Highlands and their people but learns also to admire and side with at least some of them against the government. Stevenson's novel, like Scott's, also shows us the Highlands themselves. The reader follows the heroes through the mountains and shares their experience of the landscape. We are also introduced to the clan system and the history of the Highlands in the eighteenth century.

There are however significant differences between *Kidnapped*'s portrait of the Highlands and *Waverley*'s. For a start, Stevenson's novel is set well after the defeat of the Jacobites and the Highlands in his novel are in a state of shock and depression. The clan system is still in evidence but is under threat. Although Alan Breck can usually count on support from his fellow-clansmen, he acknowledges that he cannot trust all of them and the loyalty of the rest may cost them dear. Even James of the Glens, though he does what he can to help Alan and David escape, nevertheless has also to treat them officially as criminals in an effort, however unsuccessful it turns out to be, to avoid suspicion himself. Where Scott can present a romantic view of a Highland chief giving a banquet for his followers, accompanied by a clan bard and a clan piper, Stevenson shows us Cluny Macpherson hiding in a kind of tent, fussily supervising the cooking of a few steaks for dinner.

The Highland scenery in Scott is a romantic backdrop to the action but in *Kidnapped* it becomes a test of endurance for Alan and David as they struggle across it. The mountains that Edward Waverley admires become dangerous obstacles to the heroes of *Kidnapped* and David is exhausted by his journey through them. One of the most memorable aspects of *Kidnapped* is the way Stevenson makes the reader understand the physical and emotional strain that David in particular suffers while following Alan during their flight in the heather. They are at various times baking hot and freezing cold, very often wet, usually tired and hungry and by the end David is seriously ill.

Their discomfort is made more graphic by the way Stevenson presents the Highlands as a wilderness where there seem to be very few people. Of course Alan and David are for much of the time trying to avoid inhabited places, but in Chapter 22 Stevenson deliberately sends them across Rannoch Moor, which has always been one of the most desolate places in Scotland:

> The mist rose and died away, and showed us that country lying as waste as the sea; only the moorfowl and the peewees crying upon it, and far over to the east a herd of deer, moving like dots. Much of it was red with heather; much of the rest broken up with bogs and hags and peaty pools; some had been burnt black in a heath fire; and in another place there was quite a forest of dead firs, standing like skeletons. A wearier-looking desert man never saw...

This confirms our idea of the Highlands in the novel as an empty, hostile place, which is the first impression the region makes on us when David is washed ashore on the barren islet of Earraid in Chapter 14.

Yet it could be argued that what Stevenson is describing is not the Highlands of 1751 but those of 1886. The depopulation of the Highlands between those dates, though it had begun in the 1750s, was by no means as desperate then as it became later. The prominence in Chapter 16 of the emigrant ship adds to the suggestion that the Highland Clearances are well under way at the time of the novel. Stevenson makes the Highlands seem emptier than they really were in the time of the novel, although that is how they appeared in his time, and appear in ours.

In another way Stevenson's Highland setting is of his own time. Despite the ordeal of their journey, Alan and David do have moments of enjoyment among the moors and mountains. They camp out, fish for trout, cook for themselves, tramp through the heather, spot deer and eagles, and generally do most of the things that modern hill-walkers do nowadays. It is easy to believe that what Stevenson is describing are his own experiences when travelling through the Highlands, and by his time that of course was something for tourists and holidaymakers. For the reader, if not exactly for the characters, the flight in the heather is like an adventure holiday, a strenuous and energetic hike across country in which you get close to nature and pit your wits, and your muscles, against her. For the reader in a comfortable armchair the hardships of the characters' journey across Scotland has the romantic appeal which has become the normal way of thinking of the Highlands since Queen Victoria and Prince Albert made Highland holidays fashionable.

There is another significant difference between *Kidnapped* and *Waverley*. In Scott's novel the hero is an Englishman whereas in Stevenson's he is a Scot. Edward Waverley is clearly an outsider in Scotland; David Balfour may be an outsider in the Highlands but he still thinks of himself, and the reader thinks of him, as in his own country. The division between what David represents and what Alan does is within Scotland and therefore problematic. The novel plays with the sense of the difference between Highland and Lowland Scotland, sometimes treating it as real and at other times undermining it. The difference is most apparent in terms of language. David's inability to understand Gaelic is always a handicap, as in his difficulty in realising that the man in the boat is telling him that Earraid is not an island at low tide (that the man is trying to speak English only emphasises the language barrier). On the other hand, Alan's praise of David's courage shows that Highlander and Lowlander share some qualities, and several times the point is made that Balfour is originally a Gaelic name. David's surprise at some of the things that he meets with in the Highlands is usually based on his assumption that as he is still in Scotland people and customs ought to be roughly the same.

The most important issue in this debate about whether the differences between Highlands and Lowlands are real is the nature of justice. When David is accused of complicity in the murder of the Red Fox, his first impulse is to go to the authorities and try to clear his name. He is sure that an innocent man will be treated justly. Alan, however, insists that in the Highlands justice is distorted by clan politics: 'what would the clan think if there was a Campbell shot, and nobody hanged, and their own chief the Justice General?' he says in Chapter 18. There seems to be a contrast here between Highland notions of justice, which hardly seem just at all, and Lowland ones, which David assumes are fair and true. When the story returns to the Lowlands at the end, however, we meet a lawyer who, to gain David a share of his uncle's estate, is willing to use Alan Breck the Highlander to threaten and cajole Ebenezer into betraying himself. This is not a correct legal process and its dependence on personal connections and the possibility of violence brings it closer to Highland ways of doing things than we might expect. Instead of a simple and comforting contrast between Highland 'primitive justice' and the 'civilised' legality of the Lowlands, we are left to reflect on the way both communities exploit the law for their own benefit, albeit in slightly different ways.

One aspect of difference between Highlands and Lowlands that Stevenson downplays is religion. Although the origins of Jacobitism are in the religious differences between Catholics and Protestants, *Kidnapped* says very little about this. When Alan wants to insult David he will call him a Whig, an insulting nickname for a Protestant, but David hardly seems to notice. His objection to playing cards with Cluny Macpherson is the only matter of principle that affects his behaviour in the novel and is something that God-fearing Protestants of his time, and indeed Stevenson's, took quite seriously, but David himself seems embarrassed about it and it is difficult for the modern reader to see anything religious about his scruples. On the other hand, it is equally hard to notice that Alan is a Roman Catholic. In Chapter 24 David, after being with Alan for some time, says 'I was little surprised (though, of course, I would still be shocked) to see him cross himself in the manner of the Catholics', but this is in the

context of 'the story of the Water Kelpie, that demon of the
streams' and whether Alan believes in such Celtic monsters.
Alan's crossing himself to ward off the kelpie is evidence more of
superstition than of Christian faith. The novel avoids deeper
examination of religious belief.

It could be argued that this is appropriate for what is essentially
a boy's adventure story. *Kidnapped* was written for a children's
magazine and has always been regarded as a book for young
readers. Like *Treasure Island*, it has a fast-moving plot with plenty
of exciting incidents involving strongly-defined characters in tense
and often violent situations. There is very little serious reflection
and the story hurries on before the reader can ask about the
traumatic effects on its hero of the experiences he has. Stevenson
is, as mentioned above, careful to portray David's weakness and
discomfort at times, but Alan Breck passes through the same
situations with hardly a murmur — indeed, he frequently lightens
the mood with a merry quip or sardonic remark.

Nevertheless, *Kidnapped* does have solid virtues. Stevenson's
powers of description, of both settings and characters, make the
story vivid and involving. Though the underlying structure has a
fairy-tale element, with the young hero, helped by a faithful
friend, triumphing over his wicked uncle to achieve wealth and
success at the end, the particularity of the people and places in
the novel gives it realism. Stevenson's use of history and
geography grounds the fable in time and place. This in turn
makes the novel a commentary on Scotland and Scottishness. The
alliance between Highlander and Lowlander at the heart of the
book has a message for Scottish readers and the picture it
presents of the Highlands in transition and about to enter modern
times is a study of social change that is of genuine interest.
Stevenson may have been aiming at young readers, and have
reached his target audience, but that is not to say that he
underestimated them or that what he wrote does not contain
matters of serious interest, too.

Catriona

Although he had planned a sequel to *Kidnapped* before he had
finished it, it was not until 1893, seven years later, that Stevenson
published *Catriona* (pronounced Cat-REE-na, with a stress on the
second of only three syllables). In the interval much had
happened to him. After the death of his father in 1887, Stevenson,
his mother, his wife and her son Lloyd had left Britain for
America, where Stevenson found that *Dr Jekyll and Mr Hyde* had
made him so famous that he could at last secure high prices for
his work. He did not settle there, however, and in the following
year set sail from San Francisco in a hired yacht on a prolonged
voyage around the islands of the South Pacific, until he bought
some land and built a house on Samoa. There he became both the
head of a household and involved in local politics. In 1891 he
began work on what was then called *David Balfour*, a title
retained for the American edition but changed to *Catriona* in
Britain to avoid confusion with the first novel about David
Balfour, *Kidnapped* itself.

Outline

Kidnapped ends with the hero on the doorstep of the British
Linen Company's bank in Edinburgh: *Catriona* begins with David
stepping out of the bank a short time later with a bag of money.
Almost immediately he meets a young Highland girl,
accompanied by kilted servants, and boldly starts a conversation
in the street with her in which he learns that her name is
Catriona Drummond Macgregor, and that she is the daughter of
James More, a Jacobite prisoner. He also lends her sixpence,
which will give him an excuse to visit her to be repaid. Then he
hurries about more serious business.

First he goes to a lawyer he knows to be sympathetic to the
Stewart cause and arranges for Alan Breck to be smuggled out of
Scotland to safety in France. Then he visits his cousin in Pilrig
and obtains from him a letter of introduction to William Grant of
Prestongrange, the Lord Advocate, the government prosecutor in
Scotland. David then goes to Prestongrange and surrenders
himself as the boy wanted in connection with the Appin murder of
Colin Campbell, the 'Red Fox', but he insists that as a witness to
the murder he has evidence which will clear the man accused,
James Stewart of the Glens. Prestongrange is not pleased by this,
as the government wants to convict James of the Glens to put a
stop to his Jacobite activities and deter others, but instead of

arresting David Prestongrange makes him promise to keep his evidence to himself. He then introduces David to his three daughters, the eldest of whom, Barbara, takes delight in teasing the socially-awkward country boy.

Over the next few days David criss-crosses Edinburgh, visiting Catriona and the Lord Advocate's, where he is threatened and cajoled about his evidence, and further teased by Barbara, and where he meets Catriona's father, James More, and takes a dislike to him. He fears that James More will buy his freedom by changing his politics and becoming a spy for Prestongrange. David suspects he is being followed by some of James More's Highlanders and that he may be killed to stop him giving his evidence at the trial of James of the Glens. Nevertheless, when he receives a message from Alan to say he would like to see David once more before he leaves for France, David makes his way at night to a small wood north of the city. But when Alan hears David's suspicions that he is being followed he immediately insists that they must hurry away.

For a brief period, then, Alan and David go back to being fugitives, as in *Kidnapped*. They scramble across country north-east of Edinburgh to get to the coast where the ship awaits Alan but realise as they reach the dunes near Gullane that their enemies are lying in wait for them. By going further east they outflank them but have to break cover to signal the ship. As they stand on the wide beach waiting for the ship's boat, David tells Alan he is not going with him. Instead, he turns resolutely back and is immediately captured and taken to the Bass Rock, a barren island in the Firth of Forth, once used as a prison.

David is guarded by three Highlanders and a local Scot, Andie Dale. David learns that he is to be kept on the Bass until after the trial of James of the Glens at Inveraray in Argyllshire, the home of the Campbell clan. There is little to do on the rock except tell stories. Andie Dale tells the tale of Tod Lapraik, his father's rival, whose evil *doppelganger* was seen dancing like a fiend on the Bass Rock while Lapraik himself was found in a stupor in North Berwick, the nearest port. The story causes an argument between Andie and the Highlanders and David himself intervenes to protect him. He then persuades Andie that it would be safer if they took the only boat and left the Bass Rock, marooning the Highlanders on it. Andie can fulfil his orders by keeping David in the boat until the day of the trial, while at the same time sailing as far west up the Firth of Forth as possible to give David a good start in his attempt to reach Inveraray in time.

Andie agrees and sets David ashore at the head of the firth. He
dashes across Scotland to Inveraray and arrives the following
Sunday, when all the town, including the judges and lawyers, are
in church. David's appearance in the church causes a sensation but
he is too late. The trial is over and, partly because of some very
dubious evidence from Catriona's father, James of the Glens has
been condemned to death by the Duke of Argyle, the presiding
judge and chief of the Clan Campbell. When David meets the
defence lawyers, the best they can do is prepare a legal submission
protesting at the way his evidence has been suppressed, but this
has no effect, not least because David once more attaches himself
to the Lord Advocate. The whole business of David's testimony
peters out at this point in the novel. Much later, in Chapter 20, the
execution of James of the Glens is reported but it seems almost a
formality or an afterthought in the plot.

David has decided that he wants to become a lawyer. For this
the friendship and support of Prestongrange will be invaluable
and, as the Lord Advocate still seems to want to be David's friend,
David accompanies him, first to Glasgow and then to his house in
Edinburgh. Meanwhile James More has escaped from Edinburgh
Castle. Catriona, disguised in a large hat and a greatcoat and
pretending to be a shoemaker, gained admission to her father's
cell, where he took over her disguise and walked out to freedom,
leaving her inside. It is soon made clear, however, that this was a
put-up job; James's escape is his reward for co-operating with the
government and Catriona's punishment for rescuing him will be
slight. She has already become a popular heroine for her exploit.

When David returns to Edinburgh, though, Barbara Grant
makes Catriona's felony an excuse to prevent her meeting David.
Instead she acts as a go-between, as well as teaching David how to
act like a gentleman. David is bewildered by her lively and
flirtatious manner. When he leaves to go to Leyden in the
Netherlands to begin his law studies he takes an awkward
farewell of her, not knowing whether she will let him kiss her or
not. She does so boldly and with a knowing manner, the meaning
of which David only realises when he boards ship in Leith and
discovers Catriona is travelling by the same means to the
Netherlands to join her father.

Although, as a young girl travelling on her own, Catriona is
placed under the protection of the wife of one of the merchants also
sailing to the Continent, Mrs Gebbie is so sea-sick that David and
Catriona are able to spend most of the first few days at sea alone
together. In the course of conversation, however, David mentions

some letters of his which Catriona asks to see. He gives her the bundle, forgetting that amongst them is a cheeky letter he received from Barbara when he reached the ship, in which she jokes about whether David would be allowed to kiss Catriona when he met her. Catriona is offended by this, and more so when she realises just how friendly David and Barbara have been in Edinburgh. For the rest of the voyage they hardly speak to each other.

When the ship reaches the port where Catriona is to disembark, however, the sea is so rough that it seems she cannot safely enter the boat to take her ashore, although she is determined to do so. As none of the other male passengers is willing to help, David, notwithstanding the coolness between him and Catriona, jumps into the boat to help her. Once ashore he discovers why she refused to sail on to the next port and travel back to see her father: she has hardly any money. David, angry at the thought that James More has failed to fund his own daughter's journey, goes with her to find him but they soon discover that he is not there to meet them. They wander rather aimlessly around the town and as night falls David discovers his pocket has been picked and he himself now has no money at all. There is nothing to do but walk to the seaport David was himself bound for and find his contact there, who will be able to provide him with money. When, after walking all night, they reach their destination David pretends Catriona is his sister and they at last find themselves in lodgings.

They are now in a very awkward situation. Because she does not speak the language Catriona cannot go out without David, who has learnt enough French to make himself understood. Her dependence on him is total but, aware of the impropriety of living alone in a two-room flat with an unmarried girl, to whom he is strongly attracted, David becomes terrified of doing anything which might appear to be taking advantage of Catriona. He begins attending lectures in law during the day, to avoid staying in the house with her, and in the evening spends his time trying to read a legal textbook he has bought, all the time aware that Catriona has nothing to do and cannot understand why he is being so distant, especially as occasionally he lets his guard down and treats her in a normal, friendly way.

Eventually, Catriona's father turns up. He at first shows surprise and disapproval at finding her living alone with David but his need for money, most of which he spends on drink, means he allows David to persuade him to take over his place in the flat and live there with his daughter at David's expense. Then news comes of the death of David's uncle Ebenezer and James More realises that David is now the owner of a wealthy estate. James immediately suggests that David must do the honourable thing and marry Catriona, but David refuses to do so unless Catriona herself agrees. When David asks her to marry him, however, he does it so badly that she refuses. She and her father leave the town, though not before David has secretly arranged to send James More some money each month.

David now receives a visit from Alan Breck, during which a letter comes from James More, who, with Catriona, is now at Dunkirk in France, inviting David to visit them, and asking him also to bring Alan, whom James insists is an old comrade of his because they were both at the battle of Prestonpans in 1745. James says he has a proposition to make to Alan that he can only discuss personally. David and Alan go to Dunkirk and find that James More and Catriona are living in an isolated inn amongst the dunes outside the town. Alan soon takes a great liking to Catriona, and privately urges David to renew his courtship of her, but they both distrust her father, who evades their enquiries about his scheme.

The morning after their arrival David follows Catriona to the beach, hoping to have a private word with her, but instead he sees her meeting with an officer from a ship that he recognises as HMS *Seahorse* of the Royal Navy. It seems that James has lured Alan to Dunkirk so that he can be captured and taken back to Britain for trial as a Jacobite rebel. David however speaks to Catriona as she leaves the beach and they quickly come to a better understanding of their feelings for each other. But then Catriona confesses her own suspicion of her father and shows David a letter addressed to James More that she has just received from the naval officer. She presses David to open it. He refuses, but at that moment Alan joins them and he has no hesitation in opening the letter, which confirms that James has indeed betrayed Alan.

They rush back to the inn, where Alan confronts James with his treachery. High words are followed by drawn swords and despite David's attempts to intervene the two Highlanders fight until Catriona, pushing between them to stop the duel, is accidentally wounded by David as he tries to separate the duellists with his sword. The fight ends and James More leaves the inn. Fortunately Catriona's wound is not serious and she joins David and Alan, who has taken possession of the money James had been paid to betray him, and they all escape to the town. They ride on to Paris, where David and Catriona are married. James

More has also come to Paris and when they visit him they find he
is ill in bed but quite ready to forgive them and accept the
marriage. Four days later he is dead. The novel closes with a brief
summary of the return of David and Catriona to Scotland and of
their married life together.

Structure, Characters and Themes
Unlike *Treasure Island* and *Kidnapped*, which each have one
basic plot that gives those novels a straightforward structure,
basically a journey away from the starting point and a return to
it, *Catriona* has two plots, neither of which is very satisfactory.
The first plot is the continuation of the historical element of
Kidnapped, the Appin Murder, into David's attempts to give
evidence at the trial of James of the Glens so that justice is done.
If we are aware of the historical fact that James was in fact
hanged we know that David's attempt to save him is futile. Even
if we do not know that, we probably feel that his evidence is not as
strong as he thinks and that his chances of giving it, let alone
persuading the court of James's innocence, are slight. This makes
David's efforts in the first part of the book seem a lot less
significant to the reader than they are to him.

Indeed, David only gets as far as he does because of the tolerant
attitude to him taken by the Lord Advocate. In *Catriona*, as in
Kidnapped, much of the story revolves around David's changing
relationships with men old enough to be his father. Although it is
true that Prestongrange does not want David's evidence
interfering with the conviction of James of the Glens, whose death
has already been decided upon by the government, it is not clear
why Prestongrange does not have David arrested as soon as he
reveals his identity and instead befriends him and even
introduces him to his daughters, however useful that is to
Stevenson in providing a means for David to learn how to be a
gentleman. Prestongrange has to play an awkward double role as
both the agent of the injustice done to James and the means by
which David rises in society.

Another character with an awkward double role is Catriona's
father, James More, who, as well as having a minor part in the
trial plot, also has a part in the second plot, the courtship of his
daughter by the hero. As a Jacobite turncoat James is an
unattractive figure and almost from his first appearance is made
to seem shifty and weak, and yet he is the heroine's father and
has to be respected by her and treated with some respect by David
because of her. In the second part of the novel he becomes an

embarrassment to readers and characters alike, and perhaps also to the author, who in the end disposes of him without ceremony.

James More may serve as a link between the two plots but this contributes to the unsteady impression made on the reader by Catriona herself. Stevenson introduces her to the reader as soon as possible after the novel begins but then she is kept in the background as he deals with the first plot, the trial of James of the Glens. Because of the autobiographical first-person narrative structure of the novel the reader can never see Catriona except through David's eyes but throughout most of the first half or more of the novel he himself has only fleeting glimpses and other people's accounts of her. By the time we reach Part II of the novel, consisting of only ten of the thirty chapters, which deal with the courtship of Catriona, if it may be called that, in Holland, we have only a sketchy notion of the heroine. Her most vigorous action, the daring rescue of her father from prison, is recounted to us very much at second hand and in addition is made to seem a counterfeit. The Lord Advocate allows her to set James More free because it suits the government to let him go. Catriona thus seems to have been duped into doing what he wanted and appears as much under Prestongrange's control as David is when he is detained on the Bass Rock. She certainly appears as much under the control of Prestongrange's daughter Barbara as David in the weeks before they leave for the Netherlands.

Part I gives the reader little assurance of the independence of character in Catriona of the sort needed to sustain interest in her in Part II, the period when she is living alone and isolated with David in the Netherlands. This is a very difficult part of the novel for the reader, especially the modern reader. Why are David and Catriona both incapable of telling each other what they really want? Why does David act so dishonestly to himself and to Catriona, and why is she so unable to understand him? Stevenson has deliberately put his lovers in a situation which the modern reader must suppose is improper for their time or his, but however conventional we imagine David or Stevenson's Victorian readers to be it is hard to credit the tangled mess that he makes of his relationship with Catriona at this point, and our uncertainty about her does not help.

It is not that Stevenson could not have made her spirited enough to find a way round David's obtuseness, since in Part I that is exactly what Barbara Grant does. One of the problems with the courtship plot is that David seems to be after the wrong girl. The witty and perceptive Barbara is so much more lively

than Catriona, who, as mentioned above, is kept out of sight for
most of the book, so that it is Barbara who impresses the reader.
Catriona has every justification for her jealousy of Miss Grant,
but it might have been better if instead she had tried to copy her
rival. One cannot imagine Barbara's allowing David to bury his
nose in Heineccius.

Despite these weaknesses of plot and character, there are good
things in *Catriona*. The scenes on the beaches, when Alan is
escaping from Scotland in Chapter 13 and when the action comes
to a climax outside Dunkirk in Chapter 30, have strong atmos-
phere. David's spell on the Bass Rock is also memorable, especially
for the tale of Tod Lapraik, with its powerful use of Scots and its
eerie suggestion of the doubleness of evil, an idea which might be
extended to consideration of other aspects of the novel, such as the
characters of the Lord Advocate and James More and the nature of
law and government itself. Finally, it is noticeable how much more
pacy the story becomes when Alan Breck appears in it, recapturing
some of the excitement of *Kidnapped*.

There is perhaps a way of explaining the unsatisfying general
effect of *Catriona*. The novel begins where many end, indeed
where *Kidnapped* ended, with the hero securing wealth and fine
prospects. He is at the top of good fortune and perhaps the only
way for him to go is down. As David himself says at the start of
Chapter 3:

> It seemed I was come to the top of the mountain only
> to cast myself down; that I had clambered up,
> through so many and hard trials, to be rich, to be
> recognised, to wear city clothes and a sword to my
> side, all to commit mere suicide at the last end of it...

He is of course referring to the risk he is going to take in turning
himself in as a wanted man but what he says hints that
Stevenson is writing, if not entirely a backwards romance, an
anti-novel, then one which goes against the usual direction.

Seen in this light some of the unsatisfactory aspects of the
novel make some sense. David sets out to bring justice to the trial
of James of the Glens but in the end is quite easily outwitted by
the lawyers. He makes a reckless dash across Scotland from the
Firth of Forth to Inveraray, but arrives too late to have any effect.
He makes a fool of himself in society more often than not, and is
always saying the wrong thing to Catriona and Barbara. He is
easily manipulated by Barbara, as in the farcical episode in

Chapter 20 when she allows him to see Catriona from a window, but has locked him in so that he cannot get out to meet her. Although David solemnly undertakes to act as Catriona's protector in the Netherlands, he keeps letting down his own guard on his feelings and getting himself into ridiculous situations, as with the flower he buys for her in Chapter 24. Altogether David is not very heroic and often the victim of circumstance, sometimes ludicrously so.

Much of the novel is in fact about embarrassment, as much for the reader as for the characters. Almost all the characters do or say things they regret, or have to go back on. Even the bravest and most romantic character in the novel, Alan Breck, spends most of his time running away. Stevenson certainly has a message for us about the trickery of lawyers and the dangers of becoming involved in politics but it is not a very heroic one. Having had some experience in Samoa of political manoeuvring and the unpleasant consequences of violent disputes, he was in *Catriona* less inclined perhaps than in *Kidnapped*, or *Treasure Island*, to romanticise action and adventure but instead showed the limits of individual intentions and ambitions. If so, he was doing a dangerous thing, for few readers can avoid disappointment with a novel that sets out to revise the conventional expectations of historical fiction.

CONCLUSION

The novels discussed in this book have several things in common. All three of them are told in the first person by one of the main actors in the story. They all involve journeys into places strange to the narrators and adventures in those places. In each novel the hero is young and inexperienced and not only needs to rely on older people, almost all men, but also wants to rely on them, and yet in each novel the older men often prove unreliable and even untrustworthy. The men whom the heroes rely on most, Long John Silver, Alan Breck and Lord Prestongrange, are paradoxical figures, admirable in some ways but open to suspicion in others. Silver is the most extreme combination of good and bad and Prestongrange the most difficult to understand. Alan Breck is the most reliable and his fallible side is the least dangerous. The general view of the world in the novels, however, is remarkably cautious. Stevenson presents us with a world of perils for the unwary, where it is hard to find true friends. To survive means being suspicious and as self-reliant as you can, although this makes it difficult to find friendship and, as *Catriona* shows, love. *Treasure Island* and *Kidnapped* are novels of adventure, and *Catriona* is too, if in a slightly different way, but they are not set in a shallow world of thoughtless action for the sake of excitement alone. They pose serious questions about the individual's responsibilities to society and to the self.

SELECT BIBLIOGRAPHY

1. Books by Robert Louis Stevenson:
Travels with a Donkey (1879) and *The Amateur Emigrant* (1895),
edited by Christopher MacLachlan (Penguin Classics, 2004).
Treasure Island (1883), edited by Emma Letley (World's Classics
[now Oxford Classics], 1985).
The Strange Case of Dr Jekyll and Mr Hyde (1886), edited by
Martin A. Danahay (Broadview Literary Texts, 1999).
Kidnapped (1886) and *Catriona* (1893), edited by Emma Letley
(World's Classics [now Oxford Classics], 1986).
The Master of Ballantrae (1889), edited by Adrian Poole (Penguin
Classics, 1996)
South Sea Tales, edited by Roslyn Jolly (World's Classics [now
Oxford Classics], 1996).

2. Books and articles about Robert Louis Stevenson:
Bell, Ian, *Robert Louis Stevenson: Dreams of Exile* (Mainstream
Publishing, Edinburgh, 1992). A modern biography.
Fowler, Alistair, 'Parables of Adventure: the Debatable Novels of
Robert Louis Stevenson' in *Nineteenth-Century Scottish Fiction*,
edited by Ian Campbell (Barnes and Noble, New York, 1979), pp.
105-129. Includes some detailed comment on *Treasure Island*.
Furnas, J. C., *Voyage to Windward* (Faber and Faber, London,
1952). The standard biography of Stevenson.
Maixner, Paul (ed.), *Robert Louis Stevenson: The Critical Heritage*
(Routledge and Kegan Paul, London, 1981). The publication
and early reviews of Stevenson's major works.
Robson, W. W., 'The Sea Cook: a Study in the Art of Robert Louis
Stevenson' in *On the Novel*, edited by B. S. Benedikz (J. M.
Dent, London, 1971), pp. 57-74. On *Treasure Island*.
Sandison, Alan, *Robert Louis Stevenson and the Appearance of
Modernism* (Macmillan, London, 1996). Good chapters on
Treasure Island and *Kidnapped* and *Catriona*.
Vogler, Christopher, *The Writer's Journey: Mythic Structure for
Storytellers and Screenwriters* (Michael Wiese Productions,
Studio City California, 1992). Narrative structure explained
and illustrated, though no mention of Stevenson.

3. On-line information:
The Robert Louis Stevenson Web Site
http://dinamico.unibg.it/rls/rls.htm
Much information about Stevenson with links to other sites.

One Book One Edinburgh

In February 2007, City of Literature will launch Scotland's first citywide reading campaign, One Book One Edinburgh. Thousands of free copies of Robert Louis Stevenson's *Kidnapped* will be distributed around the city. There will be a variety of support events at schools, libraries and venues in Edinburgh to encourage everyone to join in with events and celebrate Stevenson's work by picking up and reading a copy of *Kidnapped*.

Edinburgh is the world's first City of Literature – a unique, permanent designation conferred by UNESCO in 2004 in recognition of the Scottish capital's rich literary heritage, dynamic present and bold aspirations for the future.

The City of Literature trust works to promote Scotland and its literary life, proclaiming the profound importance of words, ideas and literature to Scotland, its connections with the world and its future.

The trust provide a focus and co-ordination for literary activity, encouraging greater participation and attracting new initiatives. It is also working to develop an international network of cities of literature.

To read more about why Edinburgh is the first UNESCO City of Literature, or learn about forthcoming literary initiatives and book events, visit www.cityofliterature.com for the full story.